Poetic Notions

Poems

Wade Newsom

JACKET ART
Sharon Newsom — sharon@ithreegd.com | ithreegd.com

BOOK DESIGN AND LAYOUT
Sharon Newsom

AUTHOR'S PHOTO CREDIT
Lewis Cooper — gonzoshots.com

KICKSTARTER VIDEO
Micah James

ISBN-13: 978-1502401083
ISBN-10: 1502401088

FIRST EDITION: October 2014

no·tion

ˈnōSHən/

noun

noun: **notion**; plural noun: **notions**

1. a conception of or belief about something.

2. an impulse or desire, especially one of a whimsical kind.

For Mom and Dad —
You stand beside me in the places where even angels find fright.

And for my wife Sharon, for helping me find the poet.

I want to swim in the deepest lives, in the waters most swift.

~ PABLO NERUDA

CONTENTS

IN THE WORDS

This is where it makes sense to me
In the words
I swim in them
Sometimes the hurt shows
But like the river I'm swimming in
The words always flow

PARTICIPATE

Get lost in this moment
Let this moment foment a riot inside of you
Close your eyes so that you can truly see
Be inspired by the sense of your own mortality

Participate in your existence

Let down your walls of resistance
And give your heart a beat

Let the air that escapes your lungs
Become a song that will be sung
For generations to come

Give your breath a voice

This is what was meant to be
And I'm doing what I was meant to do
So sit me down inside of you
And let me see this world
From your point of view

Let this poem be the air that keeps you breathing
Let these words be the truth that keeps you believing
Let us reconsider our conveniences
Because that $hit can be deceiving

Living lies often leads to paralysis
But truth be told
The truth often suffers from too much analysis

So trade in the known for the unknown
And be willing to take a fall
Because the point is to make your point
And if you can't make your point

What's the point of it all?

A million people with nothing to say
Still equals nothing at the end of the day

And without a voice ...

poof

Life
Painted every color of every beat
With a fleet of faith
Carrying you over those walls of resistance

Participate in your existence

Believe me when I say
If there is just one person
In just one place
Who's brave enough to stand up
And occupy even just one space

Then you and I should be able to
Wipe the sweat from our brow
And the fear from our face
And dance on top of the sweet sounds
Of sister faith

Ride this heartbeat of bass from my brother time
And I should be able to open up myself to you
And let you become the inspiration
For the words of my rhymes

Participate in my existence

▶

Help me peel away these layers of indifference
That I wrap myself in

Put the key in the lock of the box
And unlock the notion
That there is more to life than just surviving

Start striving
To live your life
The way that you see

Don't worry about being perfect
Because the movement
Doesn't have to be

MY PEN. MY GUN

Between my finger and my thumb
Rests my gun
Loaded with endless capabilities
I fire soliloquies
And just to show my versatility
I write rhymes of different kinds
Some of which are blessed with fertility
Giving birth to this hope that we can suppress the hostility
And bring about tranquility

All of these rhymes in my mind
Help define where I'm at in this space and time
My pen spells out the words that I struggle to say
And it's through these words that I find my way
Exposing my sadness
Exposing my gladness
Exposing my madness
My literary literally exposes my humility
Especially when the insanity is pulling me from reality

My pen takes me to places that I've never been
Deliberately delivering me to find something within
She takes my hand and together we move in total nonchalance
Gliding across the page she likes to flaunt
The curves of the words she leaves behind
And when the two of us get together with a bottle of wine
There's a real good chance that we're going to conceive
A real good rhyme

She leads me to her bed of white
We do it in the dead of the night
Pages upon pages until we get it right
It's only when I stop trying to impress my peers

▶

And I address my fears
That I can put something out to let you in
Express upon the page the mood I'm in
The black ink the Yang
The white page the Yin

My pen
Is my gun
Loaded with resolve and solution
And together the two of us
Are going to write a revolution

ROSE GARDEN DREAMS

Some people see the world
As a Rose Garden Dream
Yet keep their distance
For fear of the Thorn

But until you've been pricked
By pain, or love, or fear
You'll never feel realness
Or smell the sweet scent
Of your Dreamy Roses

DOVE WRAPPER HAIKU

Believe in yourself
Take a deep breath and exhale
Treat yourself today

POETS AND PROPHECIES AND GHOSTS

The father of Frisco poetry
Prophesied our genocide

He did so with a Howl

Lamb-like youth packed the Six Gallery
To watch barriers fall under City Lights

The minds of the underrepresented outcasts
Slowly destroyed by madness
While the heavy-headed hipsters
Steal our beards and drink our beer

So ...
We drink wine
And smoke marijuana with angels

Staggering on tenement roofs
Peering out through the windows of our skull
Cool radiant midnight streetlight
Shining down on sanity
Sitting on the benches we once occupied

Shaking with shame in our shadows
Life butchered out of their own bodies
Insanity is ecstasy
Dreams! Visions! Miracles!
Casting clocks off the roof in favor of eternity

Wondering where to go
Then going
Breaking bread over the broken hearts
Of those left waiting in the midnight solitude

▶

Ghostly daze of dead-end alleyways
Whereas our highways rock 'n roll
With joyrides in stolen nights

We were expelled from sanity
For baring our souls and publishing odes
But our hopeful hallucinations
Became the power behind your prose

SHINE

Suddenly it's real
The ink is on the line
And it hits harder
Than I expected

Rehearsal time is over
The spotlight shines
On the great weight
Of bleary time

Sold the keys
So I'm breaking into revelation
Ready to dip into new days
Eyes dispatched
Looking for second takes

New beginnings
Begin and end
First with the right
Then with the left
Always moving up — down

Set to sessions
Casting dream dust to destiny
Where names are written next to royalty
On the world's highest beam

The sky begs for more stars
Someone to shine

Shine Poet

Shine

DRAPED IN SECRETS

The moon cuts a path for us to see
The black waters of the night part
To make room for the real darkness

Wading through this wasteland
With steadfast faith
Breathing the shadows of lost loved ones

Their scent swirling the quiet past into life
They live in me now
In memory

In moments when I'm lost
They find me
Reminding me

Of why I'm here

GOING BLIND

Hickory hands cradle my head
While my mother's ready-to-drop eyes
Gaze from a hospital bed
Being born is going blind
And I've been born a thousand times

WEAPONS OF MASS CREATION

A stick of dynamite on the tip of my tongue
One slip of the lip can light the fuse
Never use the words for destruction
But sometimes you've got to make noise
When poised and placed properly
Words can bring down walls
Barriers fall and channels open up for us all

Weapons of Mass Creation
For which there is no citation
You can not handcuff my words
Speech is free
Censorship is the shit that's costly
Possibly one of the worst crimes on humanity

When you tell your story
Do so with ambition
Those that think it needs censorship
Don't have to listen

This is a mission of sorts
More than a right
A necessity
It's the stories that bring out the Truth in me
And truthfully
Without the whole story
We lose half of our history

A curse cast before a jury of blurry eyes
As the lies go undetected
It's the future that's affected
So it's no mystery
Why we keep repeating our history at an alarming rate

Can anybody give me the last date
When the United States was not involved in a war

It's time to light this fuse
Let sparks spit shots at their charades
Burn down blockades
Put the bulls back on parade

The master of ceremony snatches candy from kids
Sippin' on spiked Kool Aid
The camera frames catch the spectacle
Monopolized
Disguised as a choice
A silent play in the shadows of yesterday
Trying to slip through into tomorrow unnoticed
Without making too much noise
Like one hand clapping

It's happening
The poets are exposing the politricks
The apocalypse is now
Time to take the power
Back

PIED PIPER OF THE TREE

For you sir
With the wine-soaked teeth
The one standing silently
Like the bottle from which you drink
I'll make it simple for you
Mind is the Maker
I thought it was the tree
But as I sat beneath it waiting
Eternity outlasted me

NOTEBOOKS

Notebooks filled with pages upon pages
Of thoughts and emotions from different phases
And different stages of my life
Lines of ink leading me back to a place and time
Where I learned to lose my mind to find my faith

A time when life was a maze
Days spent staring at a distant hope
Trying to touch it, feel it, drink it like water from a glass
To quench this thirst for more

Unaware of the affair that I was having with death
Life remained debonair — gentle and courteous
Impervious to self pity and obliquity
Life was being played out in the key of melodrama
Where the good is better than good
And the bad is pitch perfect black
Where ignorance is bliss and common sense lacking

I hear the life outside of these walls that I've built
To see it I need to let go of the guilt
Tilt the odds in my favor
Lose the diabolical vices and savor this day
Go to that place that I've been trying to stay away from most
Open up my eyes and face my ghosts

A past filled with memories burned
A future full of lessons learned

NEON BISCUIT

The night we stood in front of 2000
The Doc put the clock on count
Disco balls dropped on diamonds
Floating in 95 proof

Cheap resolutions and
Expensive champagne
Passed around the ball
Like joints in project halls

I still don't know the words
To the song
But the feeling from the 95
Is proof that I sang along

The stage was laced
With moonlight pearls
It was poetry in a night
Where the stars needed a mic
To be heard

Brother One and Sister Fun
Took center stage

The corners were occupied
By the Bobby Dazzlers from NYC
Checking out the Mamis from Miami
Swinging from gold ropes around their neck
Offering penthouse views
From the dance floor

Twelve o'clock
The bass line dropped
And I swear Jesus himself
Jumped off the wax
To get his boogie on

IF I RAN THE CIRCUS

Take a dip into my daydream
Leave your analytical mind
And your ego behind
Surrender to the Now

IMPERFECTION

Flint turns to flame

Smoke clouds my brain

The shake rolled tight

Tonight

My words aren't dictated by what's wrong or what's right

Tonight

It's just a matter of what feels right

Stepping outside of self arrest

A test to see if I can really slip the cuffs

Enough

Too much time spent searching for perfection

Each section it's own imperfect piece

Makes the whole piece

Perfect

FAST CAR

On the road with the roof rolled back
I've never seen a girl with a smile like that
Sit back and give this girl a stare
Let's take a fast car to who knows where

Not a care in the world I've got nothing to prove
Zero to sixty then we hit the cruise
Nothing to lose everything to gain
Now I see what it's like to be living free

Let's flee to the border 'till we hit the next city
Finally see what it means to be living
Been trying to get away since the age of 16
Have you seen how a dream looks on the big screen
It's like city lights that stay on past dark
Or the spark that you lit when you touched my heart
I've got a feeling that we belong
Together forever this is more than a song

Put the pedal to the floor
And let the wheels start spinning
I'm beginning to think you're afraid of the open road
And stories untold
I'm giving you a choice and I hope you'll come
You and me baby you're the only one

You wanna drive fast well I'm down with that
I've got my hand on the wheel
You've got your head on my lap
Looking at the stars as the world goes by
We'll take a fast car to the end of the night
Hoping one day that we can get away
Searching for that place where we can find our way

They say true love is far from reality

New day, new life, new Nationality

I don't care just as long as you're there

Let's take a fast car ride to who knows where

We've got the top rolled back

And the wind in your hair

Not a care in the world

And we're almost there

All the way west until we hit the One

Sunshine in your face we'll be having some fun

You and me baby

We're the only one

JACK AND WILL

Jack and Will went up the hill
To sit for a while underneath the stars
Hand in hand Jack asked his man
"Would you be so kind as to marry me?"

Will's knees got weak
(He almost fell down and broke his crown)
As Jack reached into his pocket
And started fumbling around

Out with a ring
It was just like a dream
Jack beamed
And Will screamed:

"Let's go to the pub
for Coronitas in a tub,
and dance a mariachi
to celebrate our love!"

On their way there
They were stopped with a stare
And a word that cuts like a knife

"Fags!"
Blindfolded and gagged
Punched and stabbed
Jack reached for Will
But all he could grab

Was air

Will fell down
In his own blood he drown
And Jack went tumbling after

They were only nineteen
Trying to start a life
When the dream was carried away
By the hands of strife

This isn't a rhyme meant for a nursery
As cursory investigations fail to reveal
The real roots of these crimes
It's time we acknowledge
It's not a phobia of homosexuality
In reality it's ignorance and insecurity
That leads to senseless brutality

BLIND FAITH

I dared to dream but they told me no
Fragile and perilous, let them go
They said a lot of things but I still believe
I can do anything if they just let me be

Nighttime fades and a brand new day
Brings hope for a future filled with love and peace
A brand new lease for those in need
It's the dream that gives me the strength I need to believe
The strength I need to proceed
Take my hand and I'll lead the way
What lies ahead is a better day

Sing a song so loud that they have to hear
Let them know what it's like to shed a tear
For the ones that we've lost and the ones that we find
Still fighting in a war that we've left behind

Give sight to the blind
Let them know it's time to live life
With an open mind

We learn by living
So live
We get from giving
So give
Fate loves the fearless
So fly

The sky is the limit so it's no surprise
I've got my head in the clouds
My eyes are wide open
Focused on the future
Bright

Everything we say and do
Will eventually come back around
The sounds — a song for our soul
The rhythm — we control

2015

Step inside
the mortar
of a firework
as it explodes
into hot ash
and golden air.
Be magnificent!

SPEECHLESS

The poem is on my lips
A kiss to set it free
A whisper
Carried on the wings
of 10,000 bees

A LOVE STORY

When our eyes first met
From across the room
The sea of people slowly sank
Into the sands of solitude

All alone and free
In the soft sands of the beach
By the sigh of the sea

The virgin stars
Reflecting on the warm outer channels
Of your cool flow

A gaze burnished by the frosty dark
Illuminating a smile framed in full lips and cherry cheeks

I dip into your baby blues and
Feel the echoes
Of your heartbeat in my chest
Bouncing off of every beat
Filling the empty spaces with sparks

When the smoke clears
I see your features in my reflection
And I recognize
I can be the sounds of my own song
But I can't be the lyrics too

So sing
Keep this dream
Between you and me
Let day long duets
Turn into infinity

Listen to the key
Unlock the harmony

Haven't you ever wanted to get away
Slip inside of a slow blues song
Ride the wave

If you saw me falling
What would you say

The day fades
The sunset splits the horizon

I hear that dreams only last until dawn
So hold tight to the song
That we flung into the night
Squeezing until our words go blind

My tongue too tight for the truth
If the dream dies
So do I

The lyrics on my lips
turn to ice — melting
A new sunrise dries my eyes
And I realize the music is still playing

No sooner than the sun set
I had a song for you
Sink into Muddy Waters
Forget the day
Let's runaway to who-knows-where

I'll bring my pen & paper
To capture the moments
So when we are old and forgetful
We can read the greatest love story
That was ever written

SAUDADE

I close my eyes
My conscience comes alive
Highs and lows like a tide
I drown in dreams
That I carry with me
Into the new day

The barbed wire that binds my wrists
Slowly slips through your grip
I am bound by the echoes
Of my own silent screams
My ears are tuned to the whispers
Carried on the clouds
Of those that have drifted away

I have held death
The last exhale of a dying breath
Has slipped through my fingertips
Like drops of rain

There will never be enough water
To quench this pain

DEVIL'S DREAMS

I've seen inside the Devil's dreams
I've seen the suffering
I know exactly what it means

The vision:
A train running through my brain
This pain
Makes it hard to sleep

The world closes in
Eyes draped in velvet curtains
Swallow it whole

Like a thief
It tries to steal my soul

Letting darkness grow
As if I need it's palettes
The blackness glows

Graveyards open up their arms
And let me in
I've been here before
But I can't remember when

SAFE RETURN TO SILENCE

Afraid to sleep
For fear of what the dream may bring
Desperate are the calls that come late at night
Ringing in your head

Out of the walls comes the banging
That the shadows keep
In the distance during the day

Pause to see if it's the sound of a heartbeat
Or footsteps in the halls

Best to yield to the traffic spilling from my head
Lights turn from green to red
Thoughts are stop and go
It seems as though the thoughts I wish would stay
Are the thoughts quickest to fade away

It's the nights that I dream in rhyme
That I awake only to find
Static on the brain waves

Rhymes fade
As a new day kicks in the door
Sleep leaps from the porch

The world rushes in to water the words
That were planted the night before
Death disguised
Found its way in again

Sitting in somber silence
Shaking thoughts from my head
Trying to catch them with cupped hands
Watching as they spill out onto pages

Words born from storms
Placed in an oarless boat
Searching for a safe return
To silence

SEEDS SOWN

Dreams of trees moaning
Branches break and blood spills stories
Of suicides to sad trees
Seeds sown on stones
Watered with tears
Roots grown
Life begins again

Lying awake counting what-ifs
Dwelling in the dark
Asking for deliverance
A spark of madness to hold on to

SEESAW

Life is like a seesaw
See I saw it up one time
And I see it down some times too
Saw the way you were looking at me
As I was looking at you

I see it for what it is
If I saw it for anything else
I wouldn't see it like a saw
Cutting right through it all

Up with the highs
Down with the lows
Looking for balance
To see if I can forget
The things that I saw

SWEET DREAMS

She keeps his words
Locked beside her bed

On certain nights
She slips them between the sheets
To lie beside her

Thin lines on pages from the past
Become blurred by gentle whispers
Erasing silence in the air

Feelings floating over you
Captured by heat and hunger
A gasp of sweet surrender
Passion playing its hand

The tip of the tongue
Taking a trip down and around your body
Accentuating every curve of every word
He ever left for you

Perhaps these are more
Than just words and blank pages and blurred lines
Perhaps the syllables alone say more
Than could ever be expressed in a single breath
Perhaps ...
Dreams really do only last until dawn

SYMPHONY OF SOUNDS

Smoke stacks stretch
From tired brick buildings
Standing tall
Like proud soldiers of the city

Watching as the world below them
Flows thick like lava

Streets filled with candied dreams
Screams
Of unforgotten souls
Melodic
Beautifully chaotic

The subway sounds of a kickdrum
Rising from the streets
Loose wheels carrying a cart
Keep a steady high hat

Horns hit
Like a breakbeat paradise
Making me Dizzy like Gillespie

The beggar's cup
Shaking like a rumba

Inside
The maestro conducts
With a steam wand baton
Adding frothy notes of Rosetta

Unpitched percussions being tapped out

Heel to toe

Heel to toe

Heel to toe

The entire Borough

Is banging out beats

For the streets to dance to

61 LOCAL

Brooklyn's embrace
Took this faceless poet
And gave me a place to rest
To test my mettle

Amongst Brownstones and broken dreams
Echoed with screams
Of unforgotten souls
Being resurrected by Truths

Hittin' harder than Broadway's bang
The city's slang like a foreign tongue
But in spots like the Bowery and the Nuyorican
Everyone is speakin' the same language

From urban and spiritual
To confessional and political
When the silver tongue stories
Fall from the lips
And hit the ears
The barriers disappear

Words ring
Like summertime thunderstorms sing
Washing over our tongues
A taste of rain mixed with the sun

Romantic rhetoric dispersed by the wind
The poems mend the space between
The silence and the song
The space where we are all one

MONKEY WRENCH

I'll be a monkey
Before I let you throw a
Wrench in my plan

A PARDON OF SORTS

I took solace in false prophets
Who promised me change but did more of the same
You dared me to dream
But my dreams are fragile things that should not be disturbed
Be careful what you provoke
You shook me
And when I awoke
I awoke to a society surviving on benzos and coke

Built to sanitize me
Trying to make me be
The me that you want me to be
When I'm just trying to be — me
But that's not always easy
My ideologies of optimism don't always set me free
I get stuck in this passing time
Uncorking memories like cheap bottles of wine
Watering my soul

The pen hits the pad and the feelings flow
Deep into this repository of dreams
Placing them on wings of hope
Setting them free

If for nothing else
Than to be able to chase those dreams
To live a life as it was meant to be
So forgive me society
But after all it was you who dared me to dream
Your wish just became my pardon

BIRTH OF A POEM

The cooking of words

Spitted on whittled sticks

Over trashcan contained flames

Grease drips

Smoke carries

Wisdom, wit, and a little bit of bullshit

Up to the sky

Collecting in the clouds

Waiting for the storm

Wind whips in the clap of a consonant

Rhymes rain down

Hurricane consequences sent

For swimming in the tidal waves of our own thoughts

OKLAHOMA

Your strength and faith are courageous

Your love contagious

580

Some of my favorite joints
Are a blend of Jazz and Hip-Hop
It moves me
Soothes me
Guru and T-Bone Shorty
Gettin' their two-step on the one
The beats melt the wax
The beats —
Like bell bottoms
Tight with flair
B.H. Linc-Dog smooth
My groove
For the shady five-eighty

COUNTRY CLUB KID

Some of the kids would sign me in as their guest
Straight to the country club
From the streets
Cannon-ball cool off in the hundred plus degree heat

We'd eat five dollar Mars Bars
And wash them down with suicide sodas

Never paid for from our pockets
Put it on the parent's tab —
Country Club Kids don't worry about money
Kind of funny
How someone's blood can turn into someone else's honey

Lines of lounge chairs cradled cocoa buttered bodies
Those bikini clad cuties had me falling in love several times a day
For some summertime hours I was living a dream
Country Club Kids were kings with coat tails
And I had hitched a ride

I got lost in those days
But sooner or later the smoke always clears
From the magic mirrors
Reality sets in and I hear that voice again
Telling me:
"Life, it ain't no Country Club kid."

HOOP DREAMS AND HIP-HOP

Stories found in loose-leaf
Written in kamikaze cursive
Verses that bleed from a born in the middle child
A wild child

Growing up in a city that's too small to be big
And too big to be small
Wild becomes the one size fits all

Solace found in broken bottle black tops
Laced with hoop dreams and hip-hop

Burnt back yards
Turned into Madison Square Gardens
Budding hope with every killer crossover
And fadeaway J

Faded T's and hand-me-down jeans
Safety pins for cuffs tailored
Chuck Taylors
A swoosh drawn on the side
To make 'em look like Nikes
(We called 'em psyches)

Spending more time learning the x's and o's
Than the p's and q's
The fuse always short
The game always long
Hardwoods played the only song
The only beat that I could hear

DISORDER

Thankful for the teachers who
wrote this restless kid's name on the board
in bright white

Those were the first moments
I envisioned my name
written in bright lights

ACT I

Letters fall from my pen to paper
Like leaves being blown from a tree
Words begin to take shape
Sentences form
Voices in my head start to escape
Thoughts are born

Curious notions swarm
Inside my head
Breathing life into a soul
That once was dead

Sippin' KoolAid from a cannon
Sucking the pleasure out of pain
Finding beauty in something as simple
As the artwork being born from a coffee stain

Trying hard to believe
In the reality of charity
And kindness and neutral tranquility
Love and ecstasy

These words being born
Set me free
Keeping me on the right side
Of that fine line that defines reality

I tend to write a lot about my sadness
Maybe it's because I'm proud of my madness

Don't get me wrong though
This isn't a cry for sympathy
Each piece of my life
Makes up the symphony

My sonata has yet to be played to the end
The concord of sound doesn't always make sense
But it is my attempt
To render beauty without burden

Act 1 is over
Please drop the curtain

CHEROKEE AVENUE
For Luca Little

I sat at the edge of the asphalt
Waiting for the tide to subside
The shadows of our childhood
Danced before me
And then jumped a train for a free ride

The sun falls behind another moon
And soon another story fades
Days turn to decades
Memories buried
But I dig you too much to ever just let them lie

What I remember most about that first day
Is how you blew in like the fast winds
Filling up a hollow home
And cutting through my bones
Anxiety covered me like an ozone

We were 7, maybe 8 at the time
Young in most minds
But old enough to know how to throw stones
And use words to break bones

We emptied pockets full of fists
And exchanged fire
But before the sun could peel itself off of the horizon
Our bond became bulletproof

Proof that some aspects of life are prioritized by chance
Sometimes the wind blows with such certainty
That you have no choice but to feel it

Often times when the wind whips
And cries fall from the sky
I think about my friend Luca
The sun on his sleeve
His heart in his hands
Always love lingers

Thoughts linger
Thoughts linger
Thoughts

Linger

I can't place my finger on the last time we spoke
I could place my finger on the phone to un-break the broke
But don't want to choke on the words
That I've swallowed for so many years
I don't want to have to fight back the tears
That I know will come

I don't want to have to say I'm sorry
For leaving you alone on the side of the road
Or for ever taking you there in the first place

I'm afraid of the stale air
And the stares that will come
When I look at myself
Through these red velvet eyes

Reconstructing moments in life
May seem pointless, in vain to some

▶

Knowing that a few small words
Can't compare to the life-sized memories
That came from the trials
The miles that we walked in each other's shoes

The smiles that carried the secrets —

We didn't drop them then
No point in dropping them now

We were 7, maybe 8
Our fate, chosen by the wind

The heart can't always define what it feels
But we try
Fortified by the sun's example
We rise

The ties that bind us
Will never let this … die

TWENTY-SEVEN

Twenty-seven is the year they go

I dodged that bullet

But now I know

Nobody gets to choose their fate

I cheated death

I missed that date

Cards down

Chips in

I'm all in because I play to win

CONFESSIONS

Can we all confess
That before the rest
Came love

Togetherness can only better us
There is cleverness in tenderness
A touch never rushed
Trust and companionship
Is what makes a relationship

So forgive me when I disagree
If you try to tell me
That guys should only fall for girls
And girls just for guys
Let's open our eyes
Erase the face of lies

Normality is only a formality
For those that choose to sit on the balcony
Of their ivory towers

Enlighten the ones that are living the fake
Decipher the reasons why the message won't take
Those that do comprehend
Will again begin to dream

Stop believing it's hopeless
Let superior motives light your way
Like a votive

They've lost themselves
Looking for the answer
As a result
We've all been exposed to their cancer

Their cigarette's silhouette pirouette
In the sky
Through the smoke
A look from elegant eyes
Telling irrelevant lies

Ignorance thrives ... Only if we let it.

UNCONDITIONAL

Pierced butterfly soil
Hearts flutter
Black blood drained from her veins
Mist falls from her eyes
An upside down reflection fades
Into another yesterday

Pines point towards the belly of our mother
She sits in spirit still
Caparisoned by sunlight and stars
Peaks rise to tickle the sky
Her eyes focused and filled with love
... it's all she knows

THE WILD

At last
I am alone in the wilderness
Thunderous thoroughfares and concrete canyons
Left behind

Time stands still
The wind rolls like waves
And whispers at the tops of pines
Wildflowers waltz in a sea of sage

The weight of sound lifted
Led by the Spirit into forbidding haunts
Well beyond the reach of civilization
Where nothing is prefabricated
There are no walls to post on
And the only thing that is super-sized is the sky

My eyes focus
Looking at the world from the stars point of view
Searching for the Truth
Lost somewhere between here and youth

The Truth
The ghost king of our dreams
Elusive — Like an outlaw on the run
Slipping away into the distant sun

So that's why I'm here
Out here in the Wild
Where the landscape of the world around me
Reflects the landscape of my heart

▶

This journey into the Wild
Is a journey into myself
Into the silence
For silence itself is a message

Waking in us something transcendent and eternal
Mythic in it's meaning
Screaming to our heart
Be Wild!
Be Free!
Believe!

ROCK-A-BYE BABY

She sings The Wabash Cannonball
Into Summertime dreams
Carried on the wings of angels
Offering a safe return to tomorrow

Rock-a-bye baby
Blowing with the wind
Songs carried away what was yesterday

At some point along the way
The dream catcher could no longer bear the weight
The bough breaks
The dreams fall
Down goes baby

Innocence and all

CHOPPING LINES

If I continue to have nights like this
I don't know that I'll be able to survive
My head is buzzing inside
Like an angry beehive

So do I write another line
To make it go away
Or do I cut another line
To make it through another day

VERSES OF THE HOLY HYMNS

Verse 1:
These words that I've inked
Are for the people of the faculties
Who seem to be impressed
By my lost soul's casualties

People criticize
They don't understand me
Thinking that they know me
Because they read some of my poetry
It's Floetry

You think you know the real me
This is my recovery
This is my discovery
Channel
My energy into rhymes
It's the cracks in the lines
Showing signs of when I gave up
Emptying my soul
Of all the life that I saved up

I plead
All the times I let them bleed me
Now they want to see me
An anti-biography
Read me

My words are not invisible
My life is metaphysical
Condensing into mythical

Let me paint you some perspective
So my words are more effective

▶

Verse 2:

Walking my streets

Is like swimming with sharks

Running from the light

So I can stay in the dark

It's a stark world but before I go out

I've got to blowout one more flame

In the corner of my brain

To try to quiet some of the voices

That are making me insane

The monster no longer lives under my bed

It's taken up residence inside of my head

Simpleminded people like to point the finger

To bring it to a close

As if death was their role

I stole

A dance from the joker's wife

Now I sing a song that was written with the joker's knife

Verse 3:
I was 18 with a .25
Thinking it would make me feel so alive
While life was swerving in and out of broken lines
I realized there was nowhere to hide

Madness washed away my sadness
The chemicals are identical
They're all the same
When you pour in a glass
And take it straight to the brain

Writing about this shit
Makes my life sound draconian
Verses of the holy hymns fit for the Smithsonian

Learning to love the pain that comes with life
Trying my best to stay away from strife

Now my lyrics are the spirits that I'm sipping on
Trying to stay calm around a ticking time bomb

WASTELAND

Underneath this smile lies pain

A wasteland full of lies, anger, and shame

I make myself a prayer

To put out the flames

Try not to focus on the past

Just for today

I am free

I might lose my faith

I know it's just one thing

But the one thing I need

Never to erase

Breathing insecurity

I admit

I used to try to kill love

But I couldn't kill it

If I couldn't feel it

FIREFLIES

Huddled in my own thoughts
My mind scatters
Like fireflies at dawn

With the new sunrise
I put it back together
With eyes closed
And notebook open

Phrases as fresh as children
In beginningless times
But familiar

A forgotten song
Floating across the water
Like waves of eternity
From a past life

BRUCE LEE OF LOOSE LEAF

I was kidnapped by ninja poets

Who taught me how to work words

Like nunchucks

And slay paper dragons

With liquid swords

AN OCEAN AND A DREAM

Touch this scar on my face
So you can feel my pain
Slip inside my brain
See the world through windows
Pain

Feel a heartbeat out of control
A soul
As dark as shadows fading in and out
With each breath lost

Push and pull
Revolving doors
Ending up right back in between
An ocean and a dream

A seam in between
The bullet and the barrel
A life in peril
Like the ocean deep
Where water is heaving

Ghosts are breathing
Wind into sails
Bells toll
Sound-waves crack the ocean
Carrying me into darkness
Filling me up like a fog
Trickles of sweat swell to rivulets

▶

Wrap your thoughts around my mental
The pain in my slang falls right on the ear
Left alone for the chosen to hear

At the edge of purpose
Scaling these words like crags
Clawing through the silence unbroken
It's as if the stones were never even spoken

DUSTY BONES

Whenever the darkness pays a visit
I allow this faceless void
His walk through the halls

After moments
Sometimes brief
Sometimes seemingly never ending
Sparring over the dark closets
Filled with dusty bones
That he wishes to trade
For ripe flesh and blood

This paltry old man knows
That in my house
He is not welcome

As he goes
He leaves behind a token of his gratitude
A bottle of ink
For purpose and rhyme
With a note attached
"Until next time ... "

BLENDED WITH SALT

Take a sip
Lick salty words off of laced lips
Top shelf with a squeeze
Intoxicating words hit you
Like a blended brain freeze

THE JOURNEY

Over half way there
Dare to scare me with your doubts
Fate loves the fearless

TONIGHT

I was once told
That if you bend a breath just right
You can hear darkness in the night
So tonight I'm casting shadows
And bringing out the ghost

Because the graves are waves of memories
And the yards are the cages that we put them in
When we don't want to let go
So let go
Step into this

Tonight we are all poets
Growing into one another
Singing ourselves into each other
Like lullabies

Tonight
We dance and drink and fill up the room
Tonight we bloom
We bloom with the blood of artists
Whose pillows are stained with lucid dreams
On nights that were made for loving
Nights when the light of the moon
Keeps tomorrow's daylight from coming too soon

Tonight
When you talk to your muse
Tell her you're having a fantastic time
Tell her you like the way that she's dressed
The way she's stripteasing, fire breathing, and dancing burlesque

Blessed by dreams
I have seen the city from rooftops
And I did not jump ... Tonight

TO THE END

I'll answer your questions
With a dance
Touching on every step
Along the way

There's enough space
On the floor
For a second chance

The rhythm is
Exactly
As it sounds

Check my mindset
Adjust the volume to desired levels
Wreak head to toe havoc

Pause for a breath
Pick them up
Then put them back down

Moonwalk and march
To the pure end

All those beats
Take their toll
Still – to the end

ONE TIME

One time
In the time before this
There was the time before that
One time

But you don't need to know the time
All the time
All you really need to know is
Now is the time

SMUGGLING BOOGIE

If you had to smuggle boogie
Into the speak easy
The password would be
"Respect"

The Fedora
Draped in red light and pinstripes
Gives you a crooked-eyed
What the fuck is up?
Look

The old standards
Lead you inside
Old fashioneds
Fill your highball

The walls are consumed
With one-twos
Six strings dance on the ceiling

Word is out
You got the boogie
That good boogie
And they all want some

So you gas a few up
And sit back clean

The beat spread
Disco-fevered
The boogie jumped off
Two/four, four/four, six/eight
Half break and run baby run

THE HEAT

A fighter
Born of a borough
That's brought up legends of the ring
This young warrior
Born of a different breed
Sows seeds watered with blood, sweat, and tears

Shadowboxing inequality and stereotypes
First with the left
Then with the right
Up
Down

Set to sessions
Swinging with the rhythm of heartbeats
Echoing six generations deep
Through the seaside streets
Of Gerritsen Beach
Where one night
Can equal the rest of your life

Displaced by the world
As it comes rushing in
This warrior rises above the tide

At five foot five
This formidable brawler
Is full of Brooklyn brawn
And Irish pride
The lamb's face a disguise
For the lion inside

Wrecking balls hang from her wrist
Ready to erase
The face of doubt
And break down barriers
Built to keep her in

A back built for the burden
Holds up skies
Carrying a nation of hopes and dreams

The fight goes beyond the ring
Through burnt battlefields
And flooded streets
She marches on

Knowing that the wisp rising from a cooling wick
Will never be as sweet as The Heat from a burning flame

ROME

I spent an entire morning
In childhood
Eyes stashed in the past
Teeth biting this poem
Like the cold wind
That chews through my skin

My mind spins
As spring creeps in

Street-level shooting stars
Explode like hot ash
Into your chest
Pouring lava into puddles

Life lines up single file
And slowly marches out into the street

The sun shines on Rome
Rainbows fill my eyes
Your steady flame fades
Falling deeper and deeper
Into the Son

STATIC SENSATIONS AND
SPINNING PROCLAMATIONS

The rain taps out drumbeats
On lonely streets
Steam rises from hot concrete
A thunderclap takes me back
Filling the hollow hallways of my mind
With the melodies of memories
Static sensations and spinning proclamations
A storm is brewing
Twisted thoughts make it all a bit cloudy
The rain washes cobwebs away
This place I call home sticks with me
I carry pieces of it with me everywhere I go
It's a part of me
It's the voice that helps me sing my song
But I choose to follow the sun
As it funnels its way through the storm clouds
Searching for signs in the sky
Hints on where to find
The next stop on this ride

LOOKING BACK

I was born on Pearl Harbor day
I dropped like a bomb
Living life fit for lyrics
Of a hip-hop song

Remember back in the day
When the joints were skinny
And we used to get our weed
From your uncle Lenny

Had to crawl before a walk
Now we're dancing two-step
And that rep you protect
Was set to tape decks

I had to press rewind
On the night that we met
So I could remember everything
About the night that we met

You're like my favorite episode
Of my favorite TV show
Where did the time go
I don't know

Had a board before the whip
Grip tape kick flip
Kick push if the pool is full
Then we can skinny-dip

Hot black top
Is where we used to shoot the rock
Crazy Larry on the corner
Preaching gospel and smoking the rock

Late night
I'm waiting for your phone call
Next day
I heard you want to break it off
From your girl
Who said don't shed tears
But if you cry too long
Then I will be right here for you

Put the top down
Baby let's take a ride
Forget the bad days
Think about the good times

Making love in the back
Under the moonlight
Make it last forever
All in one night

Live it up
Cause it may not last
Come real slow
Because life goes too fast
Had to focus on the future
To forget the past
So if you want to go
Here's your hall pass

POETRY

Poetry is medicine
Injecting life into my soul
And striking lightning
Off the breath of my pulse

Poetry is the Truth
That both answers and
Poses questions

Poetry is necessary
Poetry is life
In order to sustain it
I must give it away

PHOTOGRAPHS (AND OTHER SHIT)

I keep some old photos in a shoe box under my bed
(along with some other shit that I can't seem to throw away)
What does it mean to say that I was there
Must I prove it with pictures and keepsakes

It's really just the weight of what remains
The memories fade and the edges unravel
I don't even recognize many of the faces or places anymore
If I hadn't paused for a picture
I may have passed them by unnoticed

I suppose that's how it goes

We leave tracks to remind us of where we've been
But as with most things on this earth
That have earned the right to be observed
Those tracks will soon be buried
Lost forever

Maybe that's why I keep pieces of the past
Hidden inside of a shoe box underneath my bed
(along with some other shit that I can't seem to throw away)

BEYOND THE TREES

She wore rose petal hands
And lilac lips
That blossomed into smiles
Lighting off fireworks
In her quiet eyes

Her voice
As soft as a breath from butterfly wings
But when she spoke
You could hear her heart

She lived each day
With the sweetness of honey
Her love:
Sunshine, pure and bright

She is light
Beyond the last trees

She is home
She is home

THINK ...

it's what separates us
From the backwash
That's left in the bottle
And from the people
Who preach love songs
But continue to hate

You have to think

A SUICIDE NOTE
(ON BEHALF OF HUMANITY)

I've taken it upon myself
To write a suicide note on behalf of humanity
Insanity seems to be imminent
The writing is on the wall

You may not want to read it
But whether or not you chose to see it
The truth is, you helped ink it

Living is easy with eyes closed
A rose by any other name
Would be called Denial

Breathing fiction because friction from Truth
Gets too hot to touch for most
But the ghosts come back to haunt us when we ignore them

So let's call upon the ones in office and implore them
To provide real representation that reflects the real population
Let's get back to being one nation
One world, one race

Coming together in the face of adversity
Paying for freedom doesn't buy us security
They're selling us terror and we're buying it

Yes, terrorists are tangible
But some of our biggest threats are more abstract
For instance, there are concrete facts
That show climate change poses a bigger threat than war

But we would rather drop bombs than bad habits
If you want change then you can have it
But it's not about being proactive anymore

We can't ignore that it's happening
It's not going to happen
It's happening
Right now and in a bad way

So we need to put it in the forefront of our minds
And acknowledge the time is not now but yesterday

We want to say what's on our minds
But we often feel like no one is listening
Too busy positioning us to be a world leader

When in fact, it shouldn't even be a race
But instead a collective pace

Yet they continue to place knives in our backs
And ask us to lie down
To just accept what's happening
As if the rules of paradise and living life
Don't pertain to us

We may be lost but we are still living
So lend us your false ear
Let us fill it with love not fear
Let down your defense
You don't need to fire missiles to end an argument

▶

This is supposed to be a country of the educated
Celebrated for awareness and responsibility
But we've slipped into an eradicated state
Now our fate is as foggy as the acid rain
That fills up our lifeboats

I feel like I'm drowning
Trying to keep hope afloat
I want to write a life note

If we collectively raise our voices
In support of responsible choices
This letter can be rewritten

We have the power
We don't need permission to choose happiness for us
And future generations

Let us unite
Fight for a better world
Rewrite the future
Change the tide

Rise

THAT'S WHAT SHE SAID

Love me stronger than the hate you feel for cancer
And war
And black licorice
Talk to me with a silent stare
Miss me when you're with me
Be with me
When I'm not there

— That's what she said

POP QUIZ

Commence killer advocates
For cheese
A fantastic feast of wonder
Splendid wonder

Pause casually with confidence
Fight compromise

Drift dreamily through tranquil seas
But don't jump

Your purple hair
Has my muscles feeling like
Brooklyn Bologna

Meow!

Shut up Stinger!

Pop Quiz:
What's the cat's name?

TUCKER'S WORDS, NOT MINE

Happiness is a field of tall grass

Put in your path

For you to run through

For no other reason

Than to just run through

RIGHT WORDS, WRONG TIME

The right words often come to me when I'm in the shower
By the time I grab a pen
The words are gone
Fucked off
Down the drain
Or blowing in the wind

Maybe they got a better offer
Or traded me in
Time to begin again
Time for a cigarette but I don't smoke
Time for a bourbon
Another bourbon

Time for a lucky hand
Or a hand job
Either will do

Time to stop reading other people's shit
And saying
"I can do that too"

The words make sense when they're in my head
But much harder to come by when written or said
It's like trying to get a beautiful woman out of my mind
And into my bed

TRUTH

The words faded into the fog on the mirror
All I could hear was the whiskey on his breath
The old hand of the young man
Poking my chest

You want to know the truth poet?
Well you're not going to find it there
You need to come up for air

Down there
In the fog
Hides lies
Capsulated dreams
Wedged in between worlds

You see poet
At first all you want to do is breathe
Eventually you trade life
For bloodshot eyes
And treacly sentiment

You get comfortable down there
Safe
In the depths of your own hell

It's like that sometimes

TWEED TROUSERS

The late-night tweed trousers
Are in form tonight

Notice the form

Their cigarette docked
Anchors dropped in low lights
Brass poles with wild outflows

Everything is nothing
Yet they still want more
Rising to dizzying heights
Yet they still want more

Double breast on the chest
Double scotch on the rocks
Forget the rest
For them
Emptiness is perfect

GROUPIE

She is not here for the poem

She wants her shackles broken too

Chained to this thought

This desire

This romance

This fleeing man

Who has a key but no charm for her locket

So he runs

And the further he runs

The closer he gets to solitude

Closer to himself

Closer to the clouds

SMALL AX

He spits venom
A synonym for hatred things
A snake with no fangs
Hangs on to a hiss

As empty as the skin shed left dead
In the heat of a dying day
This game of charades
No winners
Just pretenders

An open door to an empty room
Soon enough filled with lies and lows
Blood clots stop the flow
A life lived
Through other people's Polaroids

Hearts with latches locked
Beat like a broken clock
Sand fills a river Nile
Painted with vile deeds
Reading styles stolen
Reciting rhythm that can't be borrowed
Burning your hand with the same match
That you use to try to light up tomorrow

High harks quarreling with the quiet
For the Truth
Standing on a soapbox built of bones
From all the past lives you've buried

Trying to limn life
With trite phrases and two faces
But the silver tongue is sharpened
By your lies

You see
If you are the big tree
We are the small ax

A WHISPER
(OVERHEARD AT THE IRONDALE)

You walked by a fruit stand
Paying no mind
Until your mind
Was flooded with the scent of a woman

Suddenly you were compelled to turn around
To get a better look at the melons
At the fruit stand

You said with your salty lisp,
"*I need to quench my thirst*
with the sweet juice of a nectarine.
Peel back the skin
and feel the juice run down my chin,
dripping on to my chest.
Tame this hunger
with a sweet apple —
the forbidden fruit.
Tear in to it,
piercing it's flesh,
leaving seeds in it's core
before
disposing of it."

You want to tear in to it
Leave seeds in it's core
before
disposing of it

Aren't you the one
That criticizes the corner boys
For making cat calls

But this is ok
Because it's "poetry" and
You're talking about fruit right

Poetry is no place to hang
Your insecurities
But please
Don't say you're sorry
A woman's body
Is worth more than your apology

You hide behind razor-wire words
Double entendres
And poetry ...
Poetry

Whitman would have kicked your ass
Had he been there to hear
Your words fall on the ears
Of the unsuspecting mothers and daughters
Who were there
Just to hear poetry

Once you pierce that skin
You can't just wrap it up again

Your poker table talk is taboo
And you had the nerve
To sneak that shit in to the theatre
Tucked inside of a picnic notebook
Hidden under a red, white, and blue blanket
Of insecurity

My heart bleeds
For every mother, every daughter,

▶

Every grandmother, sister, niece, and wife
Who have to live a life
Knowing that 1 in every 6 women
In the United States
Will have there innocence peeled away
Their flesh torn into
And seeds left in their core
Before
Being disposed of

1 in every 6
Has to live with the memory
Of that man at the fruit stand
Every day

So every day
I will fight the ghost of that man
To prove to her
That every man
Is not the same as every other man

So tonight
When you go to sleep
With your sweet nectarine dreams
Know this:

Your salty lisp
Will be nothing more than a whisper
After you try to kiss her
And she knocks out your teeth and
Uses them for the white picket fence
That she's building
Around an apple tree
That's growing
In the tear-soaked soil
Of her garden of change

CLICK

Feeling too fat for a photo?
Fuck society
And their super-sized judgments!

INK

This is what it's like to bleed ink
Dip your brush in it
Paint me a picture of what you think
My world looks like

My soul is an open home
Only known by some
But you might recall
That the pretty ones show up late
To the ball

The halls become packed
My heart has a hard time
Hearing the beat
The lyrics hit my lips
I can no longer take the heat
My dreams are overcrowded
I can no longer sleep
I keep the cries in the background
The crashing sound
Of brain waves on stage

Raise the curtain
Look inside
My soul is untied
Tell me what you think

This is what it's like to bleed ink

THE SWEET

Depression is that misprinted line
That we read between
To define
The subject of judgment

Those that taste it don't dare let it float from the lips
A four letter word that comes with grips

Choked by disorder
Ordered to the back of the train
Where the black rain falls
On copper-colored veins

Heartbeats echo inside your brain
A rattlesnake shake in your bones
Life becomes scarred
Stories written in kamikaze cursive
Versus of solitary confinement
Remind us that we are the lonely
But not the only

Own me?

Never

DECEMBER

She wears a welfare coat
A Bible Belt
And fur-lined ghettos

Her smile comes hungry for the fast lane
She's buzzing like ghost town flies
Her eyes set on the west
With nobody by her side
Nobody left to point at and say
"*It's all because of you.*"

She looks in the mirror one last time
Before she chases herself away
The make-up under her eyes
Can't cover the traces of tears
That have fallen over the years
The cries tell a story that she can't hide

It's cold outside

She carves a poem in the mirror before she goes
Drops the devil on her tongue and makes angels in the snow

SOLDIER'S SON

I never knew the smell of your skin
I always imagined it laced with blood
Sweat and the sweet scent of love

I never saw the true color of your eyes
But even in the photographs
I recognize the humble color of hope
Hidden beneath the dark denim

I never got to feel your callused hands hold me
Did they tremble the first time you shot for Sam
Or when you took your last breath

These images are burned in my brain
A bond sewn in my heart
It beats for you still

And I wonder how it can ache so bad
Without ever really knowing
The smell
The sight
The feel
The real existence of you

PROCESS

I live a life of self expression
Translated to the page
Lately I'm paying more attention
To the sound the wind makes
As it blows through leaves on a tree

I wonder where my life is headed
Where the wind blows
And how I can place on the page
The sound I just heard
What kind of metaphor can I draw
To make a point
What can I say
And how could I say it
To make someone want to read it
And more importantly care

It's as if everything depends on this moment
These words
It must be perfect in order to be heard
My pen moves along the page
As if it were a maze
The dead ends and wrong turns
Are what keep me going
Searching
Always searching
For the right way out

BLINK

Stoplights stare at me
Five o'clock in the morning
Blink so I can go

DEATH ON A TUESDAY IN AUTUMN

I will die on a Tuesday
Just after the sun sets
As it fades, I will follow
The wind will kiss my cheek one last time
Before it carries me away

I've always imagined myself dying in the winter
But death will find me in the Fall
Fitting for the season of change

I've always been in a rush but this time
I think I'll slow down and enjoy the ride
On the flight home I'll dream of the pauses I took
Too few and far between
Just enough space for a past life

I hope to die clean with no stains left
I stopped running a long time ago
With the hope that I'll catch my last breath with confidence

The night is dressed in white and tales are told
I overheard that you can even find a few mistakes in Heaven
So I put on a smirk and a Stetson
Gather up the clouds and make way for the lightning

INTO THE LIGHT

I want to close my eyes and disappear
Jump and fall back into you
Your look is like a wave washing over me
In a moment I'm drowning

A fresh breath of innocence finds me
But flees without warning
Like the words that I never should have said

In a moment I'm old
Trying to shake the cold
I want to warm myself again
But the sun is sinking
Such a stretch from the life I used to know

I go where most find fright
To seek shelter from the storm
Shed the flames and let the water cover me
Return me to the dust that I once was

Set my body free
Like the wind in the trees
Singing songs that help me believe
The leaves whisper Truth

The sky sheds tears
A distant rain
Washing the writing off the wall
So you don't have to read the pain

The wreckage and the ruin
Fading into the sky
I don't feel like falling
But I can't turn around now

The angels have my hand
And I'm destined to fly

BEYOND THE DROP –
TWIST OF TITLES

If you want to know why
We point to the past for glue
For truth
You have to look within —
Beyond the drop

Where we tremble in the glow
Of the dark hours —
We puff waves and wait
Surfing into the mind

El Sendero Luminoso
A castle in the sky
Where lost loved ones pass by
On new ground
Led by valkyries to Valhalla

Legends survive in whisper
Names added to the list
The scene is set:
Through the lens
The explorer swims with white salmon
Down nobody's river
Towards damnation and dreams

Hidden seams and
High-line slack lines
Perched under desert sun

It's a way of life
Held together with duct tape and passion
Wedged in between lines of perspective

▶

Here
I am red
Here
Life moves in slow motion
Here
In a moment's notice
Last weekend becomes the revenge of the beast

Day turns to a night
Dressed in mission Antarctic
The stars are icicles
Taunting the Vermilion Moon

Time marches
On the road of rhythm and insight
Boxing with the fortunes of a young hitchhiker
Pointed north

The bell tolls
Fortunes turn south
And unearth the news

The news is bad
And by bad
I don't mean good Jack

To find words for what is lost
Sometimes requires falling
To be found

But angels don't sell their wings
Or their dreams
So Sally got a grant from heaven
For the party part 2
Mending the line
Making time her own

The Sunnydale kids
Know the clock's on count
The Heat beats a little harder in the streets
To get out
You gotta be about something
You gotta breathe

Coming up for air
Whenever prayer
Shocks your faith lines
And sends out static

A late night radio call
The Great Kaia sings a song for us all

HAIKU

I write poetry
It's easier to write it
When you're living it

HASHTAG YOUTH

I think I'll write a poem
For the youth of today
I'll use hashtags
And write it on a backlit screen

I'll call it "Green" and
They can read it
While they're out to dinner
With their parent

CALI BABY

Beach hoppin'
Bottle-nose poppin'
Horses runnin' down 101 no stoppin'
An 805 sip
And Airstream hip
— Cali Baby

REVELATIONS 1:1

A madman
Mad to live
Mad to dream
Mad to Be

Floating between the edge of an ocean
And reality

Dipping into daydream
Brushstrokes limn what could be
What should be

Pulling palettes bright
Out of night

Illuminating darkness
So we can see the shine

DELTA STYLE

One of these days
The trouble won't bother me anymore
One of these days
I'll leave 'em at the door

But in the meantime
Pour me some more
And if I wake up on the floor again
Forgive me
Again

HELL HOUND

He carried a compass
Code and courage
Malaria tablets
And an M-16 assault rifle
Fully loaded with 20 rounds of kill-em-all

A .45 caliber side kick for tunnel duty
Full clip

In his breast pocket over his heart
He carried a snapshot
Of his young bride
Wearing a sun dress
On a summer's day
Swinging from a swing
Hung from a Willow weeping

He carried shrapnel in his leg
Cigarettes for shot nerves and shot up friends
A single grenade —
In case shit got really bad

He carried lice and leeches and jungle rot

Nightmares

He carried the land itself
The soil
The red dust on his faded black boots
The monsoons

He carried the sky

And he carries it still

FLAMES

A bottle of wine
And some white
Lights my veins
Flames fill my body
But quickly turn to smoke and
Clouds the slippery slope

The problem provides the solution
I no longer feel the pain
For the first time in weeks
The steady drip
      drip
         drip
Fades

For the moment
Two wrongs feel so right
Tonight
I'm a slave
Tonight
I gave in
Tonight
I win

Tomorrow ...

ABSOLUT POETRY

I've got the recipe for revolution
Put it in a bottle and
Call it a solution

Pollution of minds cleaned
With black squid ink

Connect

With switchblade sharpness
Inject

Thoughts

Shot through this pen

It's the Truth for me
The words bind
My world

A spotlight for the dark
Stark naked
With an open heart

A PLACE TO SHINE

Dreamt I was a poet
Writing a revolution
What's a revolution
Without a dreamer anyway

So let me dream tonight
In the company of those
With spotlight to spare
Where hearts stay open past dark

Dreamt I was a poet
Turning water into words
And words into rhymes

Poetic phrases unfold
Like full length features
Ink plays with lyrics
The spirits sing the song

Make it last
Make it first
Make it outlast the last verse

Dreamt I was a poet
With a place to shine
Before the sun comes up
And the dreams get left behind

DANCE WITH MY POETRY

Listen
Can you hear those simple sounds
Rising up from all around

Listen
To the words ring out
Melodies carried through the air
Rising up from everywhere

Listen
Won't you dance with my poetry
Come and flow with me
Like a slow tornado
Spin around the floor with me

Your every inhale
Becomes my every exhale
You suck the air from my lungs
Leaving me with a mouth full of moth wings
Dry

Just trying to breathe
Breath
Please resuscitate me
Your mouth to mouth
Shook me
Like a magician holding a fist full of dance

Dance
With my poetry

STARRY NIGHT

Your love is like sunshine
Warm and bright
My love is like moonlight
Mostly hidden from sight

But at the right time
On the right night
Like a storybook setting
Or a piece from Van Gogh

My love opens up
And showers you in full glow

FAIRY TALES AND HAPPY ENDINGS

Morning sunbeams shadowbox with dreams
Fighting for new beginnings
Looking for fresh starts
Stuck with stale endings

It's harder than it seems
Picking up the pieces of broken dreams
Trying to cut my heart free
But it seems to be hardened by the times
That were dealt to me

I have an ace up my sleeve
So I believe
That if played properly
These pen strokes will set me free

Brush strokes and flash backs
Shaky bones and broken homes
Thunder claps and it takes me back
To that night that I held you close
You fell asleep in my arms and I swore
I would never let you go
But the lightning keeps flashing
And my eyes are stashing the memories

Half blind trying to read your mind
Losing track of time while I pick up the pieces
I'm left with traces of what used to be
Remember when you told me
That you used to fall asleep to my heartbeat

▶

What a dream we used to keep
Seems like just last week we were cheek to cheek
Now I'm losing sleep
Trying to keep the beat
This sea that I'm swimming in is never ending

I use pen strokes to float
To give birth to new life
New beginnings
Fairy tales and happy endings

YOUR CORNER

Your corner
Full of cutmen at the ready
A steady flow of heart and soul
Ready to go
Where even the angels find fright

Giving sight to blind faith
Holding your hand
When you're running with eyes closed
Through echoes of your own shadows

When the path becomes rocky
We carve stones into stories
Weaving in and out of tender and tough love
Passages wide enough for beginnings
But too tight for timid

Amid storms
We gather the gray
As the lightning comes
Making room for magnificent

In your corner

PASSION

Imagine
Today is your last day
It's your only day
Today
The pulse of your story
Will come rising up through you
And be given back to the wind

As wind whips
Fervor reaches a fever pitch
And you realize that you stitch
A pattern so bold in the fabric of time
That the colors of your story
Will paint the sky forever

What will your story be
How will you be defined
Now rewind
Imagine you're living
No longer pretending
Because pretending lacks passion
The heartbeat

Pumping vision to blood
And blood back into vision
Now my eyes are too filled with dreams
To see *without* precision

Envision
One mind
In the heart of this place

With one voice

Singing one song

That starts with a single word

Rising up to the clouds

Striking lightning off the breath of your pulse

And raining down on the rest of us

I think that song

Would sound something like

A single moment

That could lead to a million things

Like a waterfall that begins

With only one drop of water

Life is fluid

And I'm just a formless boat

Making waves

A golden tongue drifter

Who chooses to watch

The tragic sleight-of-hand

Because often times its the tragedies behind the triumphs

That really make the moments magical

Move the moments through you

Like the lightning that you become

When you find your cause

Be willing to die for the cause

But do everything you can to live for the cause

Because

You might just be

The Cause

▶

But cause without passion
Is slow suicide
Like quicksand dreams
That everyone seems
To sink their eyes into

Passion
It's out there
It's like the silent salient truth
Answering all of your questions
Without having to speak

But some people riddle rumors
About it's existence
Some people only know
Truth that's written on the walls
Of the cemeteries of originality

They liked what I said about passion
But they did so from a distance
Because in the distance
It's easy to hide
In the distance
The voodoo child on our lips
Forgets how to kiss the sky

So point me towards passion
And I will go
I will go because I know the future
Is only a breath away
And every moment I stay
Another dream dies

Stillness kills the realness

It locks dreams in dusty jars

Places them on shelves

Slanted under the weight of nevermore

Lost in time

Flatline your mind

And open your hearts

To this thing called life

Do something that's worth remembering

Life is here

365 days a year

24 hours in a day

60 minutes in an hour

60 seconds in a minute

Every moment matters

Passion is now

Passion is every second

Of every hour

And when the power of passion

Overcomes the passion of power

We will be able to see things

From the inside out

We will let the outside in

We will begin to participate again

Imagine you're living

Turn "should haves"

Into "hell yeahs"

Break open those dusty bottles
And let loose the dreams
Chase the dreams
Don't waste a moment

Because one moment
Can make a lifetime

ACKNOWLEDGMENTS

My wife Sharon — The golden twilight of your laughter brightens my day.

Mom and Dad — You stand beside me in the places where even angels find fright. Thank you for your unconditional love and unwavering support.

My brothers Gant and Clint — You keep my voice strong and my glass full.

Amy and Holly — For the collective song and the tag along.

George and Wini — For the extended love and support.

Ron and Barb — The gate keepers. Thanks for letting me in.

S.B — For the love from the other side.

Lemon Andersen — My mentor. Thanks for welcoming me into your country and sharing the stage.

The 5Point Family — For giving me a spotlight to shine.

My Crew (you know who you are) — For always holding the line steady.

Alya Howe, Michele Kiley, Justice Snow's, Poets in the Parlor, The Poetry Brothel, Steve's Guitars, Ignite Boulder, The Crystal Theatre, Aspen Writers' Foundation, Aspen Poets Society, Brooklyn Poets, Carbondale Council on Arts and Humanities, Success 3.0 Summit — All of you for sharing your stage.

SHOUT-OUTS

To catch dreams, you need a net. This book wouldn't be possible without the love and support of many. Much love and gratitude to *all* of you who had a hand in helping make this happen.

Barbara and Ron Bush

Luca Little

Coert Voohees

Wini and George Johnson

(HS)2 Program CRMS

Draper White

Heidi Johnson

Jim Noyes

Jan Koorn

Melany Boughman

Amber Tatro Leonard

Elliott Larson

Amelia, Jack, Juliet and Randy Spurrier

Tracy Wilson

Logan Carter

Sarah Wood

Johann Aberger

Richard Fuller

Joe Weinstock

Chris "C Mac" McNamara

Dalene Rankin "In Loving Memory" of Kelly Osborn

Candace Suechting

Jeff Michaud

Margaret Mathers

Alison and Nathan Nicholas

5Point Film Festival

Megan Larsen

Crystal Theatre

Sylvia Ferrero

Skip Carter

Carol Kelly

Rusty Stehr

Lila, Clara, Amy and Gant Newsom

Jamie Adamson

Patty Harkin

Isaac Savitz

Kent McKeaigg

Dr. Jason Miranov

Amy Kimberly

Joey Haack

Ken Tuitele

Craig Fulmer

Matt Haslett

Barbara Balaguer

Pam Weber

Micah James "MJ"

Jeremy Collins

Porter, Crew, Holly and Clint Newsom

Thomas Morgan

Paul LeClere

Nicole Nichols

Nate Grinzinger

William Kloster

James Anderton

Jennifer Douma

Michael Dunn

Lalanya Bingham

Herbert Feinzig

Julie and Michael Kennedy

Tucker

ABOUT THE AUTHOR

 **Wade Newsom** is a poet in every sense of the word. His sincere and adamant passion for life and living it to the fullest is obvious by the evident enjoyment he takes from performing and inspiring his audience and readers. He draws from a rich mosaic of experience that includes genuine success as a professional cyclist, an imaginative entrepreneur and an accomplished wordsmith. His poetry is moving and authentic as it evolves from Wade's deep concern for the message, the resonating sound of his syllables and the soul rocking rhythm of the delivery.

Wade's performance of his poem *Participate* at the 2013 5Point Film Festival garnered him national attention in the spoken word and performing community. Since then, he has performed at venues across the country, including readings in the birthplace of the contemporary spoken presentation, Brooklyn, NY, and in his home town, Carbondale, CO. He has often performed at readings which featured other well known poets including Tony-Award winning poet Lemon Andersen.

Wade's poetry and his spoken word performances are inspired and inspiring. They are heartfelt, poignant and thought-provoking and somehow at the same time responsive to his audience. His poems will speak to you like an old trusted friend, but will sometimes surprise you, coming at you with the weight of a sledgehammer. They will challenge you to tap into your own personal power and to live authentically by turning your "should haves" into "Hell Yeahs!".

WEBSITE wadenewsom.com

EMAIL wadenewsom22@gmail.com

16120992R00087

Made in the USA
San Bernardino, CA
20 October 2014